A SALUTE TO THE
AMERICAN SPIRIT

A SALUTE TO THE
AMERICAN SPIRIT

BRYAN CURTIS, Editor

RUTLEDGE HILL PRESS™

Nashville, Tennessee

A DIVISION OF THOMAS NELSON, INC.
www.ThomasNelson.com

Published by Rutledge Hill Press,
a division of Thomas Nelson, Inc., P.O. Box 141000,
Nashville, Tennessee 37214.

Photo on page 21 courtesy of George Bush Presidential Library. Photos on pages
39 and 93 courtesy of Library of Congress. Photos on pages 57, 75, and 111 courtesy
of National Archives.

Design by Gore Studio Inc.

Library of Congress Cataloging-in-Publication Data

A salute to the American spirit / Bryan Curtis, editor.
     p. cm.
     ISBN 1-40160-004-2
     1. Presidents—United States—Quotations. 2. National characteristics,
American—Quotations, maxims, etc. 3. United States—Politics and government—
Quotations, maxims, etc. I. Curtis, Bryan.
E176.1.S19 2002
973'.09'—dc21   2002008102

Printed in the United States of America

02 03 04 05 06 — 5 4 3 2 1

IN MEMORY OF MY GRANDMOTHER,
IRENE FOSTER

Her beautiful spirit and love of life inspired not only me,
but all who were fortunate to have known her.

PREFACE

An effective leader uses his words wisely. The quotations in this collection represent times throughout the history of the United States when our president used words to define being an American and to motivate and rally the nation's citizens. The words that have inspired Americans have become as much a part of our history as any battle, any crisis, or any milestone.

Calvin Coolidge described the feelings of most citizens when he said, "Patriotism is easy to understand in America—it means looking out for yourself by looking out for your country." Throughout our history, Americans have responded to their presidents' calls to support their country. Franklin D. Roosevelt acknowledged this patriotic spirit when he thanked Americans for digging into their pockets during World War II, saying, "And every one—every man or woman or child—who bought a War Bond helped—and helped mightily!"

Our presidents have inspired us to serve and defend our nation. Ronald Reagan motivated citizens to serve others when he said, "The work of volunteer groups throughout our country represents the very heart and soul of America. They have helped make this the most compassionate, generous, and humane society that ever existed on the face of this earth." And more recently George W. Bush rallied America to defend our freedom when he declared, "America is a nation full of good fortune, with so much to be grateful for. But we are not spared from suffering. In every generation, the world has produced enemies of human freedom. They have attacked America, because we are freedom's home and defender. And the commitment of our fathers is now the calling of our time."

I hope this book will give you a boost when times are tough and inspire you to show your patriotism and give praise to our nation, its institutions, and its leaders whenever it is due.

Patriotism is easy to understand in America—it means looking out for yourself by looking out for your country.

—CALVIN COOLIDGE

America, with the same voice, which spoke herself into existence as a nation, proclaimed to mankind the inextinguishable rights of human nature, and the only lawful foundation of government.

—JOHN QUINCY ADAMS

I believe also in the American opportunity which puts the starry sky above every boy's head, and sets his foot upon a ladder which he may climb until his strength gives out.

—BENJAMIN HARRISON

The path we have chosen for the present is full of hazards, as all paths are. The cost of freedom is always high, but Americans have always paid it. And one path we shall never choose, and that is the path of surrender, or submission.

—JOHN F. KENNEDY

The integrity of our country and the stability of our government mainly depend . . . on the loyalty, virtue, patriotism, and intelligence of the American people.

—ABRAHAM LINCOLN

Americans are generous and strong and decent, not because we believe in ourselves, but because we hold beliefs beyond ourselves. When this spirit of citizenship is missing, no government program can replace it. When this spirit is present, no wrong can stand against it.

—GEORGE W. BUSH

I see a great nation, upon a great continent, blessed with a great wealth of natural resources. Its hundred and thirty million people are at peace among themselves; they are making their country a good neighbor among the nations. I see a United States which can demonstrate that, under democratic methods of government, national wealth can be translated into a spreading volume of human comforts hitherto unknown, and the lowest standard of living can be raised far above the level of mere subsistence.

—FRANKLIN D. ROOSEVELT

Let us therefore animate and encourage each other, and show the world that a free man, contending for his liberty on his own ground, is superior to any slavish mercenary on earth.

—GEORGE WASHINGTON

And what a century it has been. America became the world's mightiest industrial power; saved the world from tyranny in two world wars and a long cold war; and time and again, reached out across the globe to millions who, like us, longed for the blessings of liberty.

—BILL CLINTON

If national pride is ever justifiable or excusable it is when it springs, not from power or riches, grandeur or glory, but from conviction of national innocence, information, and benevolence.

—JOHN ADAMS

What really proves that a person or a team or a country has it is not when it is winning and everybody is with it and everybody is cheering it on, but when it has lost one and it does not lose its spirit, it comes back, it comes back and goes on to win.

—RICHARD M. NIXON

A great people has been moved to defend a great nation. Terrorist attacks can shake the foundations of our biggest buildings, but they cannot touch the foundation of America. These acts shattered steel, but they cannot dent the steel of American resolve. America was targeted for attack because we're the brightest beacon for freedom and opportunity in the world. And no one will keep that light from shining. Today, our nation saw evil, the very worst of human nature. And we responded with the best of America—with the daring of our rescue workers, with the caring for strangers and neighbors who came to give blood and help in any way they could.

—GEORGE W. BUSH

Genius is free to announce its inventions and discoveries, and the hand is free to accomplish whatever the head conceives not incompatible with the rights of a fellow being. All distinctions of birth or of rank have been abolished. All citizens, whether native or adopted, are placed upon terms of precise equality. All are entitled to equal rights and equal protection. No union exists between church and state, and perfect freedom of opinion is guaranteed to all sects and creeds.

—JAMES K. POLK

16

That love of order and obedience to the laws, which so remarkably characterize the citizens of the United States, are sure pledges of internal tranquility; and the elective franchise, if guarded as the ark of our safety, will peaceably dissipate all combinations to subvert a Constitution, dictated by the wisdom, and resting on the will of the people.

—THOMAS JEFFERSON

A man who is good enough to shed his blood for his country is good enough to be given a square deal, because he is entitled to no more and should receive no less.

—THEODORE ROOSEVELT

In this great nation there is but one order, that of the people, whose power, by a peculiarly happy improvement of the representative principle, is transferred from them, without impairing in the slightest degree their sovereignty, in the full extent necessary for the purposes of free, enlightened, and efficient government.

—JAMES MONROE

18

And so, my fellow Americans, we must be strong, for there is much to dare. The demands of our time are great and they are different. Let us meet them with faith and courage, with patience and a grateful and happy heart. Let us shape the hope of this day into the noblest chapter in our history. Yes, let us build our bridge. A bridge wide enough and strong enough for every American to cross over to a blessed land of new promise.

—BILL CLINTON

This is America . . . a brilliant diversity spread like stars. Like a thousand points of light in a broad and peaceful sky.

—GEORGE BUSH

Allow me to say that you, as a portion of the great American people, need only to maintain your composure, stand up to your sober convictions of right, to your obligations of right, to your obligations to the Constitution, and act in accordance with those sober convictions, and the clouds now on the horizon will be dispelled, and we shall have a bright and glorious future.

—ABRAHAM LINCOLN

In a very real sense, it will not be one man going to the moon, it will be an entire nation. For all of us must work to put him there.

—JOHN F. KENNEDY

The American backwoodsman—clad in his hunting shirt, the product of this domestic industry, and fighting for the country he loves, he is more than a match for the vile but splendid mercenary of a European despot.

—WILLIAM HENRY HARRISON

A man does what he must—in spite of personal consequences, in spite of obstacles and dangers and pressures—and that is the basis of all human morality.

—JOHN F. KENNEDY

And yet we all understand what it is—the spirit—the faith of America. It is the product of centuries. It was born in the multitudes of those who came from many lands—some of high degree, but mostly plain people, who sought here, early and late, to find freedom more freely.

—FRANKLIN D. ROOSEVELT

While every American citizen must contemplate with the utmost pride and enthusiasm the growth and expansion of our country, the sufficiency of our institutions to stand against the rudest shocks of violence, the wonderful thrift and enterprise of our people, and the demonstrated superiority of our free government, it behooves us to constantly watch for every symptom of insidious infirmity that threatens our national vigor.

—GROVER CLEVELAND

The construction of the Lincoln Memorial and of a memorial bridge from the base of the Washington Monument to Arlington would be an appropriate and symbolic expression of the union of the North and the South at the Capital of the Nation. I urge upon Congress the appointment of a commission to undertake these national improvements, and to submit a plan for their execution; and when the plan has been submitted and approved, and the work carried out, Washington will really become what it ought to be—the most beautiful city in the world.

—WILLIAM H. TAFT

We Americans of today, together with our allies, are making history—and I hope it will be better history than ever has been made before.

—FRANKLIN D. ROOSEVELT

The American Dream is a song of hope that rings through night winter air. Vivid, tender music that warms our hearts when the least among us aspire to the greatest things—to venture daring enterprises; to unearth new beauty in music, literature, and art; to discover a new universe inside a tiny silicon chip or a single human cell.

—RONALD REAGAN

No nation has greater resources than ours, and I think it can be truthfully said that the citizens of no nation possess greater energy and industrial ability.

—THEODORE ROOSEVELT

Two centuries ago our nation's birth was a milestone in the long quest for freedom, but the bold and brilliant dream which excited the founders of our nation still awaits its consummation. I have no new dream to set forth today, but rather urge a fresh faith in the old dream.

—JIMMY CARTER

You know, when the framers finished crafting our Constitution in Philadelphia, Benjamin Franklin stood in Independence Hall and he reflected on the carving of the sun that was on the back of a chair he saw. The sun was low on the horizon. So he said this—he said, "I've often wondered whether that sun was rising or setting. Today," Franklin said, "I have the happiness to know it's a rising sun." Today, because each succeeding generation of Americans has kept the fire of freedom burning brightly, lighting those frontiers of possibility, we all still bask in the glow and the warmth of Mr. Franklin's sun.

—BILL CLINTON

It is a distressful time for many of our people, but they have shown qualities as high in fortitude, courage, and resourcefulness as ever in our history. With that spirit, I have faith that out of it will come a sounder life, a truer standard of values, a greater recognition of the results of honest effort, and a healthier atmosphere in which to rear our children. Ours must be a country of such stability and security as can not fail to carry forward and enlarge among all the people that abundant life of material and spiritual opportunity which it has represented among all nations since its beginning.

—HERBERT HOOVER

We have endured a long night of the American spirit. But as our eyes catch the dimness of the first rays of dawn, let us not curse the remaining dark. Let us gather the light.

—RICHARD M. NIXON

The manner by which women are treated is a good criterion to judge the true state of society. If we know but this one feature in a character of a nation, we may easily judge the rest, for as society advances, the true character of women is discovered.

—BENJAMIN HARRISON

Whatever America hopes to bring to pass in the world must first come to pass in the heart of America.

—DWIGHT D. EISENHOWER

Martin Luther King's dream was the American Dream. His quest is our quest: the ceaseless striving to live out our true creed. Our history has been built on such dreams and labors. And by our dreams and labors we will redeem the promise of America in the 21st century.

—BILL CLINTON

But peace does not rest in the charters and covenants alone. It lies in the hearts and minds of all people. So let us not rest all our hopes on parchment and on paper, let us strive to build peace, a desire for peace, a willingness to work for peace in the hearts and minds of all of our people. I believe that we can. I believe the problems of human destiny are not beyond the reach of human beings.

—JOHN F. KENNEDY

I am proud of America, and I am proud to be an American. Life will be a little better here for my children than for me. I believe this not because I am told to believe it, but because life has been better for me than it was for my father and my mother. I know it will be better for my children because my hands, my brains, my voice, and my vote can help make it happen.

—GERALD FORD

A man who has never lost himself in a cause bigger than himself has missed one of life's mountaintop experiences. Only in losing himself does he find himself.

—RICHARD M. NIXON

Where the children of rich and poor mingle together on the playground and in the schoolroom, there is produced a unity of feeling and a popular love for public institutions that can be brought about in no other way.

—BENJAMIN HARRISON

That government is best which governs the least, because its people discipline themselves.

—THOMAS JEFFERSON

That government is best which governs the least, because its people discipline themselves.

—THOMAS JEFFERSON

Why does it follow that women are fitted for nothing but the cares of domestic life, for bearing children and cooking the food for the family? I say women exhibit the most exalted virtue when they depart from the domestic circle and enter on the concerns of their country, of humanity, and of their God.

—JOHN QUINCY ADAMS

I have faith that with God's help we as a nation will move forward together as one nation, indivisible. And together we will create an America that is open, so every citizen has access to the American dream; an America that is educated, so every child has the keys to realize that dream; and an America that is united in our diversity and our shared American values that are larger than race or party.

—GEORGE W. BUSH

I know only two tunes: one of them is "Yankee Doodle" and the other one isn't.

—Ulysses S. Grant

The name of American, which belongs to you, in your national capacity, must always exalt the just pride of Patriotism, more than any appellation derived from local discriminations. With slight shades of difference, you have the same religion, manners, habits, and political principles. You have in a common cause fought and triumphed together, the Independence and Liberty you possess are the work of joint counsels, and joint efforts, of common dangers, sufferings, and successes.

—GEORGE WASHINGTON

And every one—every man or woman or child—who bought a War Bond helped— and helped mightily!

—FRANKLIN D. ROOSEVELT

———✦———

I want the people of all the earth to see in the American flag the symbol of a Government which intends no oppression at home and no aggression abroad, which in the spirit of a common brotherhood provides assistance in time of distress.

—CALVIN COOLIDGE

In the beginning the Old World scoffed at our experiment; today our foundations of political and social belief stand unshaken, a precious inheritance to ourselves, an inspiring example of freedom and civilization to all mankind.

—WARREN G. HARDING

The work of volunteer groups throughout our country represents the very heart and soul of America. They have helped make this the most compassionate, generous, and humane society that ever existed on the face of this earth.

—RONALD REAGAN

42

For I stand tonight facing west on what was once the last frontier. From the lands that stretch three thousand miles behind me, the pioneers of old gave up their safety, their comfort and sometimes their lives to build a new world here in the West. They were not the captives of their own doubts, the prisoners of their own price tags. Their motto was not "every man for himself"— but "all for the common cause." They were determined to make that new world strong and free, to overcome its hazards and its hardships, to conquer the enemies that threatened from without and within.

—JOHN F. KENNEDY

Our great resources therefore remain untouched for any purpose which may affect the vital interest of the nation. For all such purposes they are inexhaustible. They are more especially to be found in the virtue, patriotism and intelligence of our fellow-citizens, and in the devotion with which they would yield up by any just measure of taxation all their property in support of the rights and honor of their country.

—JAMES MONROE

If wrinkles must be written upon our brows, let them not be written upon the heart. The spirit should not grow old.

—JAMES A. GARFIELD

For more than three centuries we Americans have been building on this continent a free society, a society in which the promise of the human spirit may find fulfillment. Comingled here are the blood and genius of all the peoples of the world who have sought this promise.

—FRANKLIN D. ROOSEVELT

History is a ribbon, always unfurling; history is a journey. And as we continue our journey, we think of those who traveled before us. . . . Now we hear again the echoes of our past: a general falls to his knees in the hard snow of Valley Forge; a lonely President paces the darkened halls, and ponders his struggle to preserve the Union; the men of the Alamo call out encouragement to each other; a settler pushes west and sings a song, and the song echoes out forever and fills the unknowing air. It is the American sound. It is hopeful, big-hearted, idealistic, daring, decent, and fair. That's our heritage; that is our song. We sing it still. For all our problems, our differences, we are together as of old, as we raise our voices to the God who is the Author of this most tender music. And may He continue to hold us close as we fill the world with our sound—sound in unity, affection, and love—one people under God, dedicated to the dream of freedom that He has placed in the human heart, called upon now to pass that dream on to a waiting and hopeful world.

—RONALD REAGAN

Any culture which can put a man on the moon is capable of gathering all the nations of the earth in peace, justice, and concord.

—RICHARD M. NIXON

History and experience tells us that moral progress cannot come in comfortable and in complacent times, but out of trial and out of confusion. Tom Paine aroused the troubled Americans of 1776 to stand up to the times that try men's souls because the harder the conflict, the more glorious the triumph.

—GERALD FORD

So look around here, look around here. Old or young, healthy as a horse or a person with a disability that hasn't kept you down, man or woman, Native American, native-born, immigrant, straight or gay—whatever—the test ought to be: I believe in the Constitution, the Bill of Rights and the Declaration of Independence. I believe in religious liberty, I believe in freedom of speech, and I believe in working hard and playing by the rules. I'm showing up for work tomorrow. I'm building that bridge to the 21st century.

—BILL CLINTON

The hopes of all mankind rest upon us—not simply upon those of us in this chamber, but upon the peasant in Laos, the fisherman in Nigeria, the exile from Cuba, the spirit that moves every man and Nation who shares our hopes for freedom and the future. And in the final analysis, they rest most of all upon the pride and perseverance of our fellow citizens of the great Republic.

—JOHN F. KENNEDY

The Yankee intermingles with the Illinoisan, the Hoosier with the Sucker, and the people of the South with them all and it is this comingling which gives that unity which marks the American nation.

—BENJAMIN HARRISON

The Almighty God has blessed our land in many ways. He has given our people stout hearts and strong arms with which to strike mighty blows for freedom and truth. He has given to our country a faith which has become the hope of all peoples in an anguished world.

—FRANKLIN D. ROOSEVELT

I am heartily rejoiced that my term is so near its close. I will soon cease to be a servant and will become a sovereign.

—James K. Polk

The new frontier of which I speak is not a set of promises—it is a set of challenges. It sums up not what I intend to offer the American people, but what I intend to ask of them. It appeals to their pride, not their pocketbook—it holds out the promise of more sacrifice instead of more security.

—John F. Kennedy

For more than half a century, during which kingdoms and empires have fallen, this Union has stood unshaken. The patriots who formed it have long since descended to the grave; yet still it remains, the proudest monument to their memory. . . . In my judgment, its dissolution would be the greatest of calamities. . . . Upon its preservation must depend our own happiness and that of countless generations to come. Whatever dangers may threaten it, I shall stand by it and maintain it in its integrity to the full extent of the obligations imposed and the power conferred upon me by the Constitution.

—ZACHARY TAYLOR

From this day forward, let each of us make a solemn commitment in his own heart: to bear his responsibility, to do his part, to live his ideals—so that together, we can see the dawn of a new age of progress for America, and together, as we celebrate our 200th anniversary as a nation, we can do so proud in the fulfillment of our promise to ourselves and to the world.

—RICHARD M. NIXON

The great primary and controlling interest of the American people is union—union not only in the mere forms of government . . . but union founded in an attachment of . . . individuals for each other.

—JOHN TYLER

America has been the New World in all tongues, to all peoples, not because this continent was a new-found land, but because all those who came here believed they could create upon this continent a new life—a life that should be new in freedom.

—FRANKLIN D. ROOSEVELT

The capacity of the female mind for studies of the highest order cannot be doubted, having been sufficiently illustrated by its works of genius, of erudition, and of science.

—JAMES MADISON

I believe the destiny of your generation—
and your nation—is a rendezvous with
excellence.

—LYNDON B. JOHNSON

Those who first came here to carry out the
longings of their spirit, and the millions
who followed, and the stock that sprang
from them—all have moved forward
constantly and consistently toward an ideal
which in itself has gained stature and clarity
with each generation.

—FRANKLIN D. ROOSEVELT

We are a great empire. We are eighty years old. We stand at once, the wonder and admiration of the whole world, and we must enquire what it is that has given us so much prosperity, and we shall understand that to give up that one thing, would be to give up all future prosperity. This cause is that every man can make himself. It has been said that such a race of prosperity has been run nowhere else.

—ABRAHAM LINCOLN

We must remember that America cannot lead in the world unless here at home we weave the threads of our coat of many colors into the fabric of one America. As we become ever more diverse, we must work harder to unite around our common values and our common humanity. We must work harder to overcome our differences, in our hearts and in our laws. We must treat all our people with fairness and dignity, regardless of their race, religion, gender or sexual orientation, and regardless of when they arrived in our country; always moving toward the more perfect union of our founders' dreams.

—BILL CLINTON

One of the lessons taught by the late election, which all can rejoice in, is that the citizens of the United States are both law-respecting and law-abiding people, not easily swerved from the path of patriotism and honor.

—WILLIAM McKINLEY

I find also much comfort in remembering that my countrymen are just and generous and in the assurance that they will not condemn those who by sincere devotion to their service deserve their forbearance and approval.

—GROVER CLEVELAND

I am certain that after the dust of centuries has passed over our cities, we too, will be remembered not for victories or defeats in battle or in politics but for our contributions to the human spirit.

—JOHN F. KENNEDY

What brought America back? The American people brought us back—with quiet courage and common sense; with undying faith that in this Nation under God the future will be ours, for the future belongs to the free.

—RONALD REAGAN

There are millions of American men and women who are not in this war at all. It is not because they do not want to be in it. But they want to know where they can best do their share. National service provides that direction. It will be a means by which every man and woman can find that inner satisfaction which comes from making the fullest possible contribution to victory.

—FRANKLIN D. ROOSEVELT

Like a runner nearing the end of his course, I hand off the baton to those who share my belief in America as a country that has never become, but is always in the act of becoming. Presidents come and go. But principles endure, to inspire and animate leaders yet unborn. . . . That is the mission of every American patriot. For here the lamp of individual conscience burns bright. By that light, we can all find our way home.

—GERALD R. FORD

Sometimes people call me an idealist. Well, that is the way I know I am an American. America, my fellow citizens—I do not say it in disparagement of any other great people—America is the only idealistic nation in the world.

—WOODROW WILSON

Lives of nations are determined not by the count of years, but by the lifetime of the human spirit. The life of a man is three-score years and ten: a little more, a little less. The life of a nation is the fullness of the measure of its will to live.

—FRANKLIN D. ROOSEVELT

No people can live to itself alone. The unity of all who dwell in freedom is their only sure defense.

—Dwight D. Eisenhower

The country needs and, unless I mistake its temper, the country demands bold, persistent experimentation. It is common sense to take a method and try it; if it fails, admit it frankly and try another. But above all, try something.

—Theodore Roosevelt

Today, better than ever before, we know the aspirations of humankind, and share them. We have come to a new realization of our place in the world and a new appraisal of our Nation by the world. The unselfishness of these United States is a thing proven; our devotion to peace for ourselves and for the world is well established; our concern for preserved civilization has had its impassioned and heroic expression.

—WARREN G. HARDING

I want to say something to the schoolchildren of America who were watching the live coverage of the shuttle's takeoff. I know it is hard to understand, but sometimes painful things like this happen. It's all part of the process of exploration and discovery. It's all part of taking a chance and expanding man's horizons. The future doesn't belong to the fainthearted; it belongs to the brave. The *Challenger* crew was pulling us into the future, and we'll continue to follow them.

—RONALD REAGAN

America, at its best, is a place where personal responsibility is valued and expected.

—GEORGE W. BUSH

We have been, and propose to be, more and more American. We believe that we can best serve our own country and most successfully discharge our obligations to humanity by continuing to be openly and candidly, intensely and scrupulously, American. If we have any heritage, it has been that. If we have any destiny, we have found it in that direction.

—CALVIN COOLIDGE

All the extraordinary men I have known were extraordinary in their own estimation.

—WOODROW WILSON

A newly conceived Peace Corps is winning friends and helping people in fourteen countries—supplying trained and dedicated young men and women, to give these new nations a hand in building a society, and a glimpse of the best that is in our country. If there is a problem here, it is that we cannot supply the spontaneous and mounting demand.

—JOHN F. KENNEDY

Ours is a land rich in resources; stimulating in its glorious beauty; filled with millions of happy homes; blessed with comfort and opportunity. In no nation are the institutions of progress more advanced. In no nation are the fruits of accomplishment more secure. In no nation is the government more worthy of respect. No country is more loved by its people. I have an abiding faith in their capacity, integrity and high purpose. I have no fears for the future of our country. It is bright with hope.

—HERBERT HOOVER

Our strength depends upon the health, the morale, the freedom of our people. We can take on the burden of leadership in the fight for world peace because, for nearly 20 years, the Government and the people have been working together for the general welfare. We have given more and more of our citizens a fair chance at decent, useful, productive lives. That is the reason we are as strong as we are today.

—HARRY S. TRUMAN

I urge all Americans to buy War Bonds without stint. Swell the mighty chorus to bring us nearer to victory!

—FRANKLIN D. ROOSEVELT

We thereby restore the national faith, the national confidence, the national feeling of brotherhood. We thereby reinstate the spirit of concession and compromise—that spirit which has never failed us in past perils, and which may be safely trusted for all the future.

—ABRAHAM LINCOLN

Americanism is a question of principle, of purpose, of idealism, or character; it is not a matter of birthplace or creed or line of descent.

—THEODORE ROOSEVELT

Modern science has confirmed what ancient faiths have always taught: the most important fact of life is our common humanity. Therefore, we should do more than just tolerate our diversity—we should honor it and celebrate it.

—BILL CLINTON

Unless you try to do your best, unless you give everything that you have to your life and in the service of your country, then you have not been the man or the woman that you can be.

—RICHARD M. NIXON

No longer need capitalist and worker, farmer and clerk, city and countryside, struggle to divide our bounty. By working shoulder to shoulder, together we can increase the bounty of all. We have discovered that every child who learns, every man who finds work, every sick body that is made whole—like a candle added to an altar—brightens the hope of all the faithful.

—LYNDON B. JOHNSON

The poet called Miss Liberty's torch, "the lamp beside the golden door." Well, that was the entrance to America, and it still is. . . . The glistening hope of that lamp is still ours. Every promise every opportunity is still golden in this land. And through that golden door our children can walk into tomorrow with the knowledge that no one can be denied the promise that is America. Her heart is full; her torch is still golden, her future bright. She has arms big enough to comfort and strong enough to support, for the strength in her arms is the strength of her people. She will carry on in the eighties unafraid, unashamed, and unsurpassed. In this springtime of hope, some lights seem eternal; America's is.

—RONALD REAGAN

Let your heart feel for the affliction and distress of everyone.

—George Washington

It is the American story—a story of flawed and fallible people, united across the generations by grand and enduring ideals. The grandest of these ideals is an unfolding American promise that everyone belongs, that everyone deserves a chance—that no insignificant person was ever born.

—George W. Bush

The first requisite of a good citizen in this Republic of ours is that he shall be able and willing to pull his own weight.

—THEODORE ROOSEVELT

I know no safe depository of the ultimate powers of society but the people themselves, and if we think them not enlightened enough to exercise their control with a wholesome discretion, the remedy is not to take it from them, but to inform their discretion.

—THOMAS JEFFERSON

Moods come and go, but greatness endures. Ours does. And maybe for a moment it's good to remember what, in the dailyness of our lives, we forget: We are still and ever the freest nation on Earth, the kindest nation on Earth, the strongest nation on Earth. And we have always risen to the occasion. And we are going to lift this Nation out of hard times inch by inch and day by day, and those who would stop us had better step aside. Because I look at hard times, and I make this vow: This will not stand.

—GEORGE BUSH

The elevation of the Negro race from slavery to the full rights of citizenship is the most important political change we have known since the adoption of the Constitution of 1787. No thoughtful man can fail to appreciate its beneficent effect upon our institutions and people. It has freed us from the perpetual danger of war and dissolution. It has added immensely to the moral and industrial forces of our people. It has liberated the master as well as the slave from a relation which wronged and enfeebled both. It has surrendered to their own guardianship the manhood of more than 5,000,000 people, and has opened to each one of them a career of freedom and usefulness. It has given new inspiration to the power of self-help in both races by making labor more honorable to the one and more necessary to the other. The influence of this force will grow greater and bear richer fruit with the coming years.

—JAMES A. GARFIELD

The second day of July, 1776, will be the most memorable epoch in the history of America. I am apt to believe that it will be celebrated by succeeding generations as the great anniversary festival. It ought to be commemorated as the day of deliverance, by solemn acts of devotion to God Almighty. It ought to be solemnized with pomp and parade, with shows, games, sports, guns, bells, bonfires, and illuminations, from one end of this continent to the other, from this time forward for ever more.

—JOHN ADAMS

The faith of the fathers was a mighty force in its creation, and the faith of their descendants has wrought its progress and furnished its defenders.

—WILLIAM MCKINLEY

The right of revolution is an inherent one. When people are oppressed by their government, it is a natural right they enjoy to relieve themselves of oppression, if they are strong enough, whether by withdrawal from it, or by overthrowing it and substituting a government more acceptable.

—ULYSSES S. GRANT

The greatness of America has grown out of a political and social system and a method of control of economic forces distinctly its own—our American system.

—HERBERT HOOVER

In meeting the troubles of the world we must meet them as one people—with a unity born of the fact that for generations those who have come to our shores, representing many kindreds and tongues, have been welded by common opportunity into a united patriotism.

—FRANKLIN D. ROOSEVELT

The American people, entrenched in freedom at home, take their love for it with them wherever they go, and they reject as mistaken and unworthy the doctrine that we lose our own liberties by securing the enduring foundations of liberty to others. Our institutions will not deteriorate by extension, and our sense of justice will not abate under tropic suns in distant seas.

—WILLIAM MCKINLEY

To exclude from positions of trust and command all those below the age of 44 would have kept Jefferson from writing the Declaration of Independence, Washington from commanding the Continental Army, Madison from fathering the Constitution, Hamilton from serving as secretary of the treasury, Clay from being elected speaker of the House and Christopher Columbus from discovering America.

—JOHN F. KENNEDY

The institutions under which we live, my countrymen, secure each person in the perfect enjoyment of all his rights.

—JOHN TYLER

———◀◉▶———

Building one America is our most important mission—"the foundation for many generations," of every other strength we must build for this new century. Money cannot buy it. Power cannot compel it. Technology cannot create it. It can only come from the human spirit.

—BILL CLINTON

Peace, plenty, and contentment reign throughout our borders, and our beloved country presents a sublime moral spectacle to the world.

—JAMES K. POLK

The talents and virtues which were displayed in that great struggle were a sure presage of all that has since followed. A people who were able to surmount in their infant state such great perils would be more competent as they rose into manhood to repel any which they might meet in their progress.

—JAMES MONROE

For over three centuries the beauty of America has sustained our spirit and has enlarged our vision. We must act now to protect this heritage. In a fruitful new partnership with the States and the cities the next decade should be a conservation milestone. We must make a massive effort to save the countryside and to establish—as a green legacy for tomorrow—more large and small parks, more seashores and open spaces than have been created during any other period in our national history.

—LYNDON B. JOHNSON

In all our rejoicings, let us neither express nor cherish any hard feelings toward any citizen who, by his vote, has differed with us. Let us at all times remember that all American citizens are brothers of common country, and should do well together in the bonds of fraternal feeling.

—ABRAHAM LINCOLN

Tonight I ask everyone in this Chamber—
and every American—to look into their
hearts, spark their hopes, and fire their
imaginations. There is so much good, so
much possibility, so much excitement in
our nation. If we act boldly, as leaders
should, our legacy will be one of progress
and prosperity. This, then, is America's new
direction. Let us summon the courage to
seize the day.

—BILL CLINTON

Our eyes never will be blind to a developing menace, our ears never deaf to the call of civilization. We recognize the new order in the world, with the closer contacts which progress has wrought. We sense the call of the human heart for fellowship, fraternity, and cooperation. We crave friendship and harbor no hate.

—WARREN G. HARDING

But if the spirit of America were killed, even though the Nation's body and mind, constricted in an alien world, lived on, the America we know would have perished.

—Franklin D. Roosevelt

We live in an age of science and of abounding accumulation of material things. These did not create our Declaration. Our Declaration created them. The things of the spirit come first. Unless we cling to that, all our material prosperity, overwhelming though it may appear, will turn to a barren scepter in our grasp.

—Calvin Coolidge

In man's long, upward march from savagery and slavery—throughout the nearly 2,000 years of the Christian calendar, the nearly 6,000 years of Jewish reckoning—there have been many deep, terrifying valleys, but also many bright and towering peaks. One peak stands highest in the ranges of human history. One example shines forth of a people uniting to produce abundance and to share the good life fairly and with freedom. One union holds out the promise of justice and opportunity for every citizen: That union is the United States of America.

—GERALD FORD

The glory of this land has been its capacity for transcending the moral evils of our past. For example, the long struggle of minority citizens for equal rights, once a source of disunity and civil war, is now a point of pride for all Americans. We must never go back. There is no room for racism, anti-Semitism, or other forms of ethnic and racial hatred in this country.

—RONALD REAGAN

The American people stand firm in the faith which has inspired this Nation from the beginning. We believe that all men have a right to equal justice under law and equal opportunity to share in the common good. We believe that all men have the right to freedom of thought and expression. We believe that all men are created equal because they are created in the image of God.

—HARRY S. TRUMAN

I am a living witness that any one of your children may look to come here [the White House] as my father's child has.

—ABRAHAM LINCOLN

The spirit of the American people can set the course of world history. If we maintain and strengthen our cherished ideals, and if we share our great bounty with war-stricken people over the world, then the faith of our citizens in freedom and democracy will be spread over the whole earth and free men everywhere will share our devotion to those ideals.

—HARRY S. TRUMAN

Unity . . . Resolve . . . Freedom. These are the hallmarks of the American spirit. Freedom and fear are now at war, and the strength of a nation relies on the resolve and determination of its people. Our nation—this generation—will lift a dark threat of violence for our people and our future. We will rally the world to this cause by our efforts, by our courage. We will not tire, we will not falter, and we will not fail.

—GEORGE W. BUSH

I ask you to join in a re-United States. We need to empower our people so they can take more responsibility for their own lives in a world that is ever smaller, where everyone counts. We need a new spirit of community, a sense that we are all in this together, or the American Dream will continue to wither. Our destiny is bound up with the destiny of every other American.

—BILL CLINTON

This Nation was founded by men of many nations and backgrounds. It was founded on the principle that all men are created equal, and that the rights of every man are diminished when the rights of one man are threatened.

—JOHN F. KENNEDY

America is ready to encourage, eager to initiate, anxious to participate in any seemly program likely to lessen the probability of war, and promote that brotherhood of mankind which must be God's highest conception of human relationship.

—WARREN G. HARDING

America, at its best, matches a commitment to principle with a concern for civility. A civil society demands from each of us good will and respect, fair dealing and forgiveness.

—GEORGE W. BUSH

The men who mine coal and fire furnaces and balance ledgers and turn lathes and pick cotton and heal the sick and plant corn—all serve as proudly, and as profitably, for America as the statesmen who draft treaties and the legislators who enact laws.

—DWIGHT D. EISENHOWER

First in importance in the American scene
has been the inspiring proof of the great
qualities of our fighting men. They have
demonstrated these qualities in adversity as
well as in victory. As long as our flag flies
over this Capitol, Americans will honor the
soldiers, sailors, and marines who fought
our first battles of this war against
overwhelming odds—the heroes, living and
dead, of Wake and Bataan and
Guadalcanal, of the Java Sea and Midway
and the North Atlantic convoys. Their
unconquerable spirit will live forever.

—FRANKLIN D. ROOSEVELT

The war has proved . . . that our free Government, like other free Governments, though slow in its early movements, acquires, in its progress, a force proportioned to its freedom.

—JAMES MADISON

If ever there was a people who sought more than mere abundance, it is our people. If ever there was a nation that was capable of solving its problems, it is this nation. If ever there were a time to know the pride and the excitement and the hope of being an American—it is this time.

—LYNDON B. JOHNSON

We have become a great nation, forced by the fact of its greatness into relations with the other nations of the earth, and we must behave as beseems a people with such responsibilities. Toward all other nations, large and small, our attitude must be one of cordial and sincere friendship. We must show not only in our words, but in our deeds, that we are earnestly desirous of securing their good will by acting toward them in a spirit of just and generous recognition of all their rights.

—THEODORE ROOSEVELT

In the face of great perils never before encountered, our strong purpose is to protect and to perpetuate the integrity of democracy. For this we muster the spirit of America, and the faith of America.

—FRANKLIN D. ROOSEVELT

As our 200th anniversary approaches, we owe it to ourselves and to posterity to rebuild our political and economic strength. Let us make America once again and for centuries more to come what it has so long been—a stronghold and a beacon-light of liberty for the whole world.

—GERALD FORD

Let the word go forth from this time and place, to friend and foe alike, that the torch has been passed to a new generation of Americans—born in this century, tempered by war, disciplined by a hard and bitter peace, proud of our ancient heritage—and unwilling to witness or permit the slow undoing of those human rights to which this Nation has always been committed, and to which we are committed today at home and around the world.

—JOHN F. KENNEDY

You catch, with me, the voices of humanity that are in the air. They grow daily more audible, more articulate, more persuasive, and they come from the hearts of men everywhere.

—WOODROW WILSON

As a people we discovered that our Bicentennial was much more than a celebration of the past; it became a joyous reaffirmation of all that it means to be Americans, a confirmation before all the world of the vitality and durability of our free institutions. I am proud to have been privileged to preside over the affairs of our Federal Government during these eventful years when we proved, as I said in my first words upon assuming office, that "our Constitution works; our great Republic is a Government of laws and not of men. Here the people rule."

—GERALD FORD

What we need in the spirit of this country and the spirit of our young people is not playing it safe always, not being afraid of defeat—being ready to get into the battle and playing to win, not with the idea of destroying or defeating or hurting anybody else, but with the idea of achieving excellence.

—RICHARD M. NIXON

The United States did not rise to greatness by waiting for others to lead. This Nation is the world's foremost manufacturer, farmer, banker, consumer, and exporter.

—JOHN F. KENNEDY

It has been said that our best years are behind us. But I say again that America's best is still ahead. We have emerged from bitter experiences chastened but proud, confident once again, ready to face challenges once again, and united once again.

—JIMMY CARTER

I have often said that there are no two
fronts for America in this war. There is only
one front. There is one line of unity which
extends from the hearts of the people at
home to the men of our attacking forces in
our farthest outposts. When we speak of
our total effort, we speak of the factory and
the field, and the mine as well as of the
battleground—we speak of the soldier and
the civilian, the citizen and his
Government.

—FRANKLIN D. ROOSEVELT

It is, fellow-citizens, for the whole American people, and not for one single man alone, to advance the great cause of the Union and the Constitution. And in a country like this, where every man bears on his face the marks of intelligence, where every man's clothing, if I may so speak, shows signs of comfort, and every dwelling signs of happiness and contentment, where schools and churches abound on every side, the Union can never be in danger.

—ABRAHAM LINCOLN

From this day forward, the millions of our schoolchildren will daily proclaim in every city and town, every village and rural schoolhouse, the dedication of our nation and our people to the Almighty.

—DWIGHT D. EISENHOWER

Strong hearts and helpful hands are needed, and, fortunately, we have them in every part of our beloved country. We are reunited. Sectionalism has disappeared. Division on public questions can no longer be traced by the war maps of 1861.

—WILLIAM MCKINLEY

As spokesmen for the United States Government, you and I take off our hats to those responsible for our American production—to the owners, managers, and supervisors, to the draftsmen and engineers, to the workers—men and women—in factories and arsenals and ship-yards and mines and mills and forests and railroads and highways. We take off our hats to the farmers who have faced an unprecedented task of feeding not only a great nation but a great part of the world. We take off our hats to all the loyal, anonymous, untiring men and women who have worked in private employment and in Government and who have endured rationing and other stringencies with good humor and good will. We take off our hats to all Americans who have contributed magnificently to our common cause.

—FRANKLIN D. ROOSEVELT

Our country has been populated by pioneers, and therefore it has more energy, more enterprise, more expansive power than any other in the whole world.

—THEODORE ROOSEVELT

I always remember an epitaph which is in the cemetery at Tombstone, Arizona. It says: "Here lies Jack Williams. He done his damnedest." I think that is the greatest epitaph a man can have—when he gives everything that is in him to do the job he has before him. That is all you can ask of him and that is what I have tried to do.

—HARRY S. TRUMAN

If I felt that there is to be sole responsibility in the Executive for the America of tomorrow I should shrink from the burden. But here are a hundred millions, with common concern and shared responsibility, answerable to God and country. The Republic summons them to their duty, and I invite co-operation.

—WARREN G. HARDING

We have every right to dream heroic dreams. Those who say that we are in a time when there are no heroes just don't know where to look. You can see heroes every day going in and out of factory gates. Others, a handful in number, produce enough food to feed all of us and then the world beyond. You meet heroes across a counter—and they are on both sides of that counter. There are entrepreneurs with faith in themselves and faith in an idea who create new jobs, new wealth and opportunity. They are individuals and families whose taxes support the Government and whose voluntary gifts support church, charity, culture, art, and education. Their patriotism is quiet but deep. Their values sustain our national life.

—RONALD REAGAN

Our reliance is the love of liberty which God has planted in our bosoms. Our defense is in the preservation of the spirit which prized liberty as the heritage of all men, in all lands, everywhere. Destroy this spirit and you have planted the seeds of despotism around your own doors. Familiarize yourselves with the chains of bondage, and you are preparing your own limbs to wear them.

—ABRAHAM LINCOLN

Wherever life takes us, there are always moments of wonder.

—JIMMY CARTER

America is a nation full of good fortune, with so much to be grateful for. But we are not spared from suffering. In every generation, the world has produced enemies of human freedom. They have attacked America, because we are freedom's home and defender. And the commitment of our fathers is now the calling of our time.

—GEORGE W. BUSH

From now on, any definition of a successful life must include serving others.

—GEORGE BUSH

Now, each of us must hold high the torch of citizenship in our own lives. None of us can finish the race alone. We can only achieve our destiny together—one hand, one generation, one American connecting to another.

—BILL CLINTON

The problems of the world cannot possibly be solved by skeptics or cynics whose horizons are limited by the obvious realities. We need men who can dream of things that never were.

—JOHN F. KENNEDY

Don't let anyone tell you that America's best days are behind her—that the American spirit has been vanquished. We've seen it triumph too often in our lives to stop believing in it now.

—RONALD REAGAN

PRESIDENTIAL TERMS

1.	George Washington	1789–1797
2.	John Adams	1797–1801
3.	Thomas Jefferson	1801–1809
4.	James Madison	1809–1817
5.	James Monroe	1817–1825
6.	John Quincy Adams	1825–1829
7.	Andrew Jackson	1829–1837
8.	Martin Van Buren	1837–1841
9.	William Henry Harrison	1841
10.	John Tyler	1841–1845
11.	James K. Polk	1845–1849
12.	Zachary Taylor	1849–1850
13.	Millard Fillmore	1850–1853
14.	Franklin Pierce	1853–1857
15.	James Buchanan	1857–1861
16.	Abraham Lincoln	1861–1865
17.	Andrew Johnson	1865–1869
18.	Ulysses S. Grant	1869–1877
19.	Rutherford B. Hayes	1877–1881
20.	James A. Garfield	1881
21.	Chester A. Arthur	1881–1885
22.	Grover Cleveland	1885–1889
23.	Benjamin Harrison	1889–1893
24.	Grover Cleveland	1893–1897
25.	William McKinley	1897–1901
26.	Theodore Roosevelt	1901–1909
27.	William H. Taft	1909–1913
28.	Woodrow Wilson	1913–1921
29.	Warren G. Harding	1921–1923
30.	Calvin Coolidge	1923–1929
31.	Herbert Hoover	1929–1933
32.	Franklin D. Roosevelt	1933–1945
33.	Harry S. Truman	1945–1953
34.	Dwight D. Eisenhower	1953–1961
35.	John F. Kennedy	1961–1963
36.	Lyndon B. Johnson	1963–1969
37.	Richard M. Nixon	1969–1974
38.	Gerald Ford	1974–1977
39.	Jimmy Carter	1977–1981
40.	Ronald Reagan	1981–1989
41.	George Bush	1989–1993
42.	Bill Clinton	1993–2001
43.	George W. Bush	2001–